OUTER SPACE
OUTLAWS

Lorenzo Van Der Lingen

3

*GSPCM: Galactic Society for the Prevention of Cruelty to Monsters

7

Meanwhile, in the Arrival Lounge ...

On behalf of DROOG TELEVISION, I'd like to WELCOME you to our planet Mr Mantu. Gosh, I must say you're a lot BIGGER in REAL LIFE – either that or I'm a lot SMALLER! Ha–ha–ha!

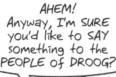

AHEM! Anyway, I'm SURE you'd like to SAY something to the PEOPLE of DROOG?

Yes.

Hello.

Aha ... RIGHT, SO – I understand you're writing an AUTO-BIOGRAPHY called "How I Saved the Universe, and Other Really Heroic Stuff"...

I BET there are LOTS of EXCITING ADVENTURES in that book you could SHARE with us ...?

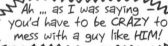

13

LOOK! I found SQUOOT!

Well, JEEVES here found him, actually. He's Saratoga's personal HELP-BOT!

GREAT! 'COS YOU'LL need HELP in a MINUTE!!

Don't you REALISE what you've DONE?!?

HEY! It wasn't MY fault! SQUOOT sat on the LAUNCH button, not ME!

NAWTY, widdle Squooty-poo! Did yew fink it said "LUNCH", my widdle baby? Hmm?

Give me strength!

Well, WHATEVER. The thing is, we have to TURN this ship AROUND and try to LAND it again!

Come on, help-bot – HELP me!

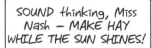

SOUND thinking, Miss Nash — MAKE HAY WHILE THE SUN SHINES!

Aw, SHADDUP!

Meanwhile, back on DROOG...

Updating our HIJACKED SPACESHIP story...

Hey, weren't the KIDS going down to that SPACE DOCK?

Shush, dear!

Police have just released IDENTIPICS of two TEENAGE GIRLS who were seen ENTERING Saratoga Mantu's SPACESHIP only MOMENTS before it was HIJACKED this afternoon.

SPACE DOCK 6

Anyone who knows the IDENTITIES of these RECKLESS TEENLINQUENTS are urged to contact the police IMMEDIATELY.

MILLIE!!

NASH?!?

Please note, these EYEWITNESS mock-ups are to be used as a GUIDE only...

My babies! My POOR babies!

Hello? Emergency? Get me the POLICE!

NO, I CAN'T call back when it's a bit less BUSY!

Meanwhile, our two "OUTER SPACE OUTLAWS" find PLENTY to do upon Saratoga's mighty vessel as it HURTLES through the cosmos...

TAG! You're IT!

OUCH!

...and MILLIE MANTU, the Empire's GREATEST monster hunter, BAGS herself yet ANOTHER trophy!

WOW, that HEAT-SEEKING LASSO is IMPOSSIBLE to dodge!

Y'know, I reckon this TRAINING ROOM is BETTER than Planet Disney!

Yeah, it's NOT BAD.

Not Bad? NOT BAD?!?

C'mon, Nash – admit it! You're having FUN!

OOf!

OW! STOP IT! Ha-ha-ha!

Kitchee-koo!

Ha-ha! OK, OK – I ADMIT it, I ADMIT it! Hee-hee!

AHEM! FORGIVE me for INTERRUPTING your high-spirited antics, but DINNER is SERVED.

PSSH

Great! Burgers and sundaes! Jeeves, you're the BEST!

Think NOTHING of it — I am DESIGNED to SERVE as BEST I can.

Um ... Jeeves — what'll happen when we get to KALGURI? Won't the Kalgurians be ANGRY when they find us here INSTEAD of Saratoga?

Possibly. But I'm SURE they'll understand that this mix-up was simply an UNFORTUNATE ACCIDENT.

But — what if they don't speak any ENGLISH?

Fret NOT, Miss Millie. Saratoga's SPARE HELMET has an inbuilt LINGUISTIC TRANSLATOR that should overcome any COMMUNICATION PROBLEMS ...

IZZAT SO?

Now, I suggest you both RETIRE to BED for the rest of our journey. I shall WAKE you when we ARRIVE.

Hmm ...

OK.

21

SLAM!

What a BULLY!

Oh, Victor, I can't BEAR to think WHAT our POOR DARLINGS are going through!

And what of the "poor darlings"?

POP

Huh? Wh— where AM I?

Oh yeah, THAT'S right.

WHAT? We've LANDED already?

Millie? Oh NO! Not AGAIN!

PSSH

JEEVES! Why didn't you WAKE me?!?

Miss Millie said you WANTED to sleep IN, I thought...

You DIDN'T think! Millie CAN'T BE TRUSTED on her OWN! Where is she?

ZIP!

Outside, talking to the Kal...

QUICK, then!

We've got to STOP her, before it's ...

And so – at the Royal Banquet Hall...

I hope you are not OFFENDED, great Saratoga...

I am SURE that the Bubble pole was FAULTY!

Don't sweat it, your Highness – my HELMET took MOST of the fall!

And at a table far away from "Saratoga"...

WHY? Why do I BOTHER, Jeeves? I should just LET her get GOBBLED up by that monster!

EXCUSE please – you no WANT?

Eh? NO, no thanks.

HEY! WAIT A MINUTE! You speak ENGLISH?!?

Oh yes! Ha-ha! English speak I WELL!

28

33

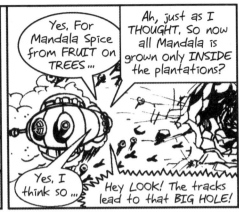

37

39

41

44

Why, merely BAGGING myself a MONSTER, sir!

Have your CONTROL CHIPS fried in the HEAT? THAT'S the monster over THERE!

EXCUSE me sir, but I BEG to DIFFER. You see, like the Kalgurians, you have become GREEDY.

Aw, come ON, Jeeves — look, any MONEY that we make EXHIBITING this monster, I'll SPLIT with you 50/50 — now THAT'S not GREEDY, is it? Whaddaya say?

I'd say, sir, that you ought to QUIT while you're AHEAD.

Eh? What do you mean?

Look BEHIND you, sir.

Oh! LORD HIGH EMPEROR! What are YOU doing here?!?

We came to see if we could HELP you, great Saratoga.

45

OK, then... but I INSIST on walking UNDER you, Millie — to CATCH you if you FALL!

Don't WORRY, Dad — I WON'T fall...

THAT only happens if you haven't done anything to DESERVE riding in one of these!

Very well, let the Parade BEGIN!

CLAP!

Hey look, Millie — BAZULE and JEEVES are UP HERE, too!

Hi!

Cool!

Hup ho!

Up they go!

Say, Nash?

Yeah?

You're no SCAREDY-CAT.

Hey, I never thought YOU WERE either!